# Three
# Presentation

Get new skills, turn nerves into energy, and deliver your best presentations ever.

## DAVID BECKETT
### Edited by Sheila Schenkel

**OVER 100,000 READERS**

*Stuart, enjoy your next pitch!*

TEDx Speech Coach David Beckett has helped hundreds of Startups to win over $30 Million in investment and over $3 Million in pitch competition prize money.

He's also trained hundreds of professionals in presentation at companies such as Philips, ING, Vodafone and Rabobank.

David enjoyed a 16 year career in international business at Canon, where he became a Country Director. 6 years ago, he became an entrepreneur and has his own Presentation Services company: Best 3 Minutes.

With *Three Minute Presentation*, David shares his extensive knowledge of how to communicate ideas to audiences of all sizes. This book offers actionable tools in short chapters that will take you less than three minutes to read, enabling you to absorb each idea and put the tools immediately into action.

David is also the creator of The Pitch Canvas©.

www.Best3Minutes.com

## Other books by David Beckett:

### Zet Jezelf Op De Kaart (Dutch)
For more info, go to PitchProfessionals.com

### Amsterdam... The Essence
For more info, go to TheEssenceOnline.com

Dedicated to Sheila for being together in Team DB, and for giving me the platform to be myself.

And a big hug for our new little'un, who was cooking in the kitchen of ideas while this book was being written. We welcome you with wide open arms and a lot of love, as we will do forever.

Thanks to;

Lance Miller, for inspiring (or was it forcing?) me to take presentation seriously over 20 years ago, and for helping me understand that 'Presentation is 9 points of the law'.

Morten Brix, for talking through our presentations over and over again.

Three Minute Presentation

Fifth edition

Written and Designed by David Beckett, Edited by Sheila Schenkel

First Published by David Beckett 2012

Copyright 2012 © David Beckett (Author) and edited by Sheila Schenkel

The moral right of the author has been asserted.

All rights reserved. No part of this book may be used or reproduced in any form or by any means without written permission except in the case of brief quotations embodied in critical articles and reviews.

For additional permissions, go to www.best3minutes.com.

ISBN – 978-1470179540

# Acclaim for David Beckett's book and presentation coaching.

"Great book! I enjoyed reading it and learning some of the best presentation tips I've ever had. It's brought me a social insight on how you present yourself, sell yourself, come across and convince. Its empowering and I am almost reluctant to share! Power of 3."
**Vincent van Duivenbooden, Ziggo.**

"David coached me from the point where I was too nervous to remember my pitch, to the moment where I pitched in front of 500 investors on stage at demo day!"
**Douwe Bart Mulder, CEO Printr**

"I find it inspiring to work according to your 3-Minute Presentation System, as well as very practical."
**Saskia Samama, Cargill.**

"In ten years of entrepreneurship, you have been the best mentor I have ever had."
**Geoffroy Simon, CEO and founder TagTag City**

"David has a huge passion for what he does. He uses his experience in pitching to help others such as myself to create and give the perfect pitch."
**Rob van den Heuvel, CEO SendCloud**

"David is excellent at capturing any audience through his outstanding presentation skills! I highly recommend him to anyone needing professional presentation coaching."
**Andrea Arlow, Canon.**

# Contents

## Introduction

| | |
|---|---|
| Why I wrote this book and how it will help you | 6 |
| The Three Minute Promise | 7 |
| Why making good presentations is important | 8 |
| The good news | 11 |

## Preparation

| | |
|---|---|
| 1. Prepare your platform | 14 |
| 2. How much time to spend on preparation | 16 |
| 3. Get started with your preparation well in advance | 18 |
| 4. Communication is what the listener does | 22 |
| 5. Assess your audience's expectations | 26 |
| 6. Know your venue and how to get there | 30 |
| 7. Focus on your delivery more than the details | 32 |
| 8. Test-drive your talk | 36 |
| 9. Use PowerPoint as a tool and consider other options | 38 |
| 10. Use the Power of Three | 42 |
| 11. Put your presentation together on Post-it notes | 46 |
| 12. Keep the details on your slides to a minimum | 50 |
| 13. Construct your slides: simple, clear, concise | 54 |
| 14. Check out the equipment at the presentation venue | 58 |
| 15. Buy yourself 10% extra confidence | 62 |
| Preparation: Summary | 66 |

## Presentation

| | |
|---|---:|
| 16. Gain confidence by visualising in advance | 70 |
| 17. Keep calm if you make mistakes | 72 |
| 18. Ensure they remember the important stuff | 76 |
| 19. Don't learn your script | 80 |
| 20. The first 60 seconds | 84 |
| 21. Use body language to express yourself | 88 |
| 22. Emphasise your message by using your hands in a conscious way | 92 |
| 23. Break through the voice barrier: listen to yourself | 96 |
| 24. Share your eye-contact | 100 |
| 25. Make it interactive once you've gained confidence | 102 |
| 26. The standing up game | 104 |
| 27. How to manage a Q&A session | 108 |
| 28. Give handouts at the end, never at the beginning | 112 |
| 29. Finish with a bang | 114 |
| 30. Follow up | 118 |
| Presentation: Summary | 120 |

## The Three Minute Presentation

| | |
|---|---:|
| 31. You really can do all this in three minutes | 124 |
| 32. Prepare an elevator pitch | 126 |
| 33. Practice makes perfect, again and again | 130 |
| Three Minute Presentation: Summary | 132 |

## Final Thoughts

| | |
|---|---:|
| Get advice and feedback wherever you can | 134 |
| Additional presentation advice and resources | 136 |

# Why I wrote this book and how it will help you

I love making presentations. Equally, I recognise public speaking is a challenge that can make many people very nervous. In fact, it can be downright terrifying.

This has led me to spend hours discussing what it takes to present successfully with numerous colleagues and friends. We've hung our heads after the horrors, when it all went terribly wrong: those were the times to make an honest assessment of what we could have improved. We've also celebrated together when it's gone well, yet still hunted for those polishings and sharpenings that could make it even better next time.

Over the last twenty years, I've coached hundreds of people and get a huge kick out of seeing them improve their presentations skills. I love seeing the kick they get out of it for themselves too.

In this book, I'm very happy to share the essentials of how to prepare, deliver and follow up on a great presentation. And finally you'll find yourself perfectly capable of giving a complete presentation in just three minutes.

# The Three Minute Promise

"It's not what you read that matters: it's what you digest and take action upon."

Modern life is hectic and none of us have the time, wish or habit to absorb large volumes of information.

I've recently thrown out a pile of (no doubt excellent) management and self-improvement books which are packed with information. Yet they're delivered in huge indigestible blocks: small type, no space for notes and covering their subject in every possible detail. The only books of this category that I went through thoroughly and took real action on were short and easily readable.

My ambition with Three Minute Presentation is to share key insights and tools in short, manageable pieces, helping you develop your skills. Every chapter will take you no longer than 3 minutes to read, and each one contains ideas that you can immediately put into practice in your daily working life.

# Why making good presentations is important

Simply because it is the single most influential activity in your career.

My conclusion after twenty years in business is that the individuals who rise to the top are, without exception, excellent presenters.

I've seen highly competent workers doing a great job every day, yet never receiving the recognition they deserve because of poor presentation skills. I've also watched average employees scale dizzying corporate heights because they have learned to present their content and (very important) themselves with impressive effect.

The same goes for entrepreneurs. Getting start-up investment comes from showing you not only have a great idea, but are also the person to make it happen. Present yourself and your idea poorly and you won't get the cash.

Is this imbalanced importance of presentation fair? Debatable. Is it true? Undoubtedly.

The obvious question to ask is this: surely a daily contribution is what matters, not shining on infrequent occasions? Why should this one skill override all others?

The answer is simple too. Whether we like it or not, we live in an age where the image is often more valuable than the true content. Each time you present, your audience is forming their own opinion about you based on what they see and hear.

Monotone delivery, reading from the screen, over-running your time and appearing unsure of your story leave the listeners feeling uncertain of your ability to carry out daily tasks. Creating memorable content, sharing the message clearly, keeping to the time schedule and delivering an inspiring talk with confidence convinces them you can do your hour-by-hour work at a high level too.

You should also be aware that if you present the work of a team, the audience invariably assumes that you are the leader and key person behind that work – regardless of whether you are the manager or not.

If you invest time and energy into improving your presentation skills, you will find your review ratings go up, and the reputation you have around the company will improve. You'll find yourself being asked to take the lead on behalf of departments and projects, giving you the limelight to shine and appear in control of the situation. All of this leads to promotion and higher earning potential.

Perhaps most of all, it will be something you can be proud of and gain personal confidence from. There is nothing quite like the thrill of hearing genuine audience applause and after-event comments of how great your story was.

In short: developing your presentation skills is an investment in every aspect of your working life.

# The good news

Anyone can learn the skills to present at an improved – and even high – level.

The other good news is that most people don't bother. They think they will be judged on results of what they do daily, regardless of whether they present well.

To be fair, that should be true. But it just isn't.

Very simply: if a decision maker has one employee with great results and great presentation, compared against another with great results and poor presentation – who is the boss going to give that promotion to?

Put yourself in the spotlight by investing time and energy into learning the skills to present, and it will pay you back tenfold.

NOTE
33 great presenters are pictured in this book. They are there as an inspiration for you to think how you might gain new ideas about communicating your ideas from the characters who do it on the highest level.

Before anything else, preparation is the key to success.

Alexander Graham Bell
(inventor)

# Preparation

# 1. Prepare your platform

When the most successful football manager in the world, Sir Alex Ferguson, took Manchester United to Barcelona or Bayern Munich for a crucial match, he didn't just let his team arrive and play. Naturally they trained in preparation.

During training he didn't shout at them, "Run faster, kick harder, pass more accurately!"

Sir Alex knew what the opposition's tactics were, how their fans behaved, how easy it was to get to the stadium from the hotel, whether the grass would be cut long or short. He'd prepare his team for every possibility, to give the players a platform to perform and demonstrate their skills at the highest level possible.

Preparing for a presentation is similar. It's not just about going over the slides a few times; it's about thinking over all aspects of those minutes that you will be in front of your audience. It's about building a platform of confidence.

This section is going to help you increase the percentages that you are going to do well, before you have said a word.

BE LIKE SIR ALEX

# 2. How much time to spend on preparation

To answer this, I'll give you my version of an apocryphal story about Pablo Picasso.

Late in life, he was stopped by a lady at an airport. Being a huge fan, she contain herself and asked the artist to make a sketch for her on a handkerchief.

Picasso did so, and handing it over to her said, "That'll be ten thousand dollars."

The woman was stunned. "How can it cost that much? It only took you thirty seconds."

Picasso looked her in the eye with a sharp piercing stare and replied, "Thirty seconds, madam, and a lifetime."

Your moments in the spotlight are the distillation of all the preparation you make. It's up to you how good you want that to be, and how much time you wish to invest into it.

There is a theory that you should spend one hour preparing per minute of allocated presentation time. This is probably excessive for most situations: nevertheless, I'd recommend investing at least 20 minutes preparation per minute of presentation.

**PICASSO'S LIFETIME**

# 3. Get started with your preparation well in advance

Usually you'll know at least a few days in advance, and sometimes longer, that you are due to make a presentation. Most people prepare like this as the days count down;

> 10 days to go: "Plenty of time to start that presentation, better just get on with this other stuff first."
>
> 6 days to go: "Really need to get to grips with that pres. I'll start first thing Monday morning."
>
> 2 days to go: "Right – everything else has to wait, I'm concentrating on that PowerPoint!"
>
> 1 day to go: "I really don't know how this is going to end up – *there simply wasn't time to prepare.*"

Life and business are busy, and you're bombarded with tasks. Nevertheless, don't be like 'most people' and avoid allowing yourself to get into that position.

I have faith in the basic principle of time-management mentioned by business coach, Brian Tracy: "There is never enough time to do everything, but there is always enough time to do the important things."

If you acknowledge that presentation can have a significant influence on your working life, then put its preparation high on your list of priorities.

As soon as you know the date of your slot, get some ideas down – even if it's just a few scribbles on pads or Post-it®*

DON'T BE LIKE MOST PEOPLE

notes (more on this later). Allowing your mind to work with the subject subconsciously is one of the best ways to prepare, and that requires time.

You'll find yourself thinking the subject over in the shower, in the car to work, and over coffee with a colleague. When those thoughts start to flow, add them to your rough notes; your story is beginning to form.

Make a quick preparation schedule so that you can manage the time up to the deadline;

  First ideas on paper/Post-its
  First draft on-screen
  Test run
  Refined version, and test
  Final edit and test

Setting up a timetable for developing the presentation to its end will set your mind at rest, and will also help ensure you prepare strongly.

## Three to remember

1. Make preparation for presentation a priority in your working day.
2. Get some content down early and let your mind subconsciously develop your message.
3. Make a schedule of different drafts and tests, so you can run through the content in advance instead of presenting 'cold'.

# A winning effort begins with preparation.

Joe Gibbs

(sports coach)

# 4. Communication is what the listener does

Before putting a word down, the most crucial element to think about is the audience.

This seems really obvious, right? Yet surely you have sat in a meeting where people tell everything in their mind, without giving a thought to how the others in the room might react.

Taking time to consider the profile of your audience and adapting the tone and detail of your message accordingly will significantly increase its impact. The basic question to answer before you start developing content is this: *What do I want the audience to do, think or say afterwards?*

A presentation is always about a persuasion. Let's compare these two sets of circumstances.

> 1. Asking the management to agree on an additional investment; convincing your team to follow a controversial strategy; introducing your products to a sceptical group of customers.
>
> 2. A project update at a weekly department meeting; a two-minute opening to a larger event; introducing yourself at a training session.

The first group consists of clear 'selling moments'. In short, you're presenting because you want to get those people to come round to your view and take action based on their agreement. It's pretty clear what you want them to do and

**WHO'S LISTENING?**

both parties are more than likely aware of the dynamics of that presentation.

The second group of situations is not so clearly about persuading or selling. Your audience is more passive, there is no overt element of bargaining, and you might just want to 'get in and get out' as quickly as possible because you are not their main focus.

However, whether we want them to or not, the audience will take action in every situation mentioned in both groups. They will form their opinion on you as a competent (or otherwise) project leader, as the guy who makes various parties feel comfortable (or otherwise) at events and meetings, and as the interesting (or otherwise) colleague that they'd like to talk with (or avoid!) at the break.

Finally every audience *will* take action, even if only in thought. Shaping that action is your role as the presenter, no matter the size of opportunity to present yourself.

## Three to remember

1. Adapt your message to the audience.
2. It's always about persuasion: sell your story, even if it's just a personal introduction.
3. They will take action in thought, word or deed. Ensure what they do is in line with your goals.

# Communication works for those who work at it.

John Powell

(composer)

# 5. Assess your audience's expectations

Part of considering your audience is taking time to assess what they are expecting. Are they looking for flamboyance? Do they just want the information, plain and simple? Are they technical people, or a mixed crowd?

Generally, this will be apparent, because the majority of presentations are given to specific types of audiences. Take this example;

> You're running a project which has an element of IT [Information Technology] transformation in it. You're not an IT specialist, but you're presenting to the managers of the IT department on the progress of the project as a whole.

Your challenge in this situation will be to ensure the IT guys realise you appreciate their job and the issues they deal with. You'll need to add some vocabulary and concepts that resonate with them: how do you do that if you're not an expert? Whatever you do, don't just bluff it! Preparation is the key.

It's clear from the beginning of the project that you'll present to various groups with an IT focus. When they contribute as the project progresses, pay close attention to their vocabulary and take time to understand to some level what their own challenges and attitudes are. Reflecting their vocabulary and concerns back to them will help you.

SURPRISE SURPRISE

In another situation you may be presenting to a more diverse team, giving you a couple of choices; go for a common denominator, or reflect as many of the relevant groups in your presentation as possible.

Here are two potential approaches;

> You're presenting to an international group of salespeople at a European head office meeting. Either present the European sales only; or mention individual countries, ensuring you name as many of the countries attending as possible.

> You're giving a talk to a group of students from a variety of disciplines who may want to work for your company. Either you focus on the general values and future of your company; or you find out exactly which subjects your audience is studying, and reflect the potential areas where they might work based on their background.

Either of these approaches will work. What's important is spending time to think the situation through.

Doing your best to reflect the audience will communicate that you care about what's important to them.

### Three to remember

1. Assess the audience's expectations.
2. Be prepared to research some concepts and vocabulary from the audience's world.
3. Make conscious decisions about how your content will match their expectations.

I don't think anyone ever gets over the surprise of how different one audience's reaction is from another.

Dick Cavett
(talk show host)

# 6. Know your venue and how to get there

One of the biggest stress-providers possible is being late. So if you're presenting at a meeting that's a 45-minute drive away, leave yourself two hours and get there early.

I know this should be obvious, but I've seen so many people arrive at the last minute, sweating as the computer fails to start up while the audience waits impatiently, that I feel the urge to push this one home.

Getting there early has other benefits. You can join the coffee break and have a chat with a couple of attendees: tell them you're presenting and looking forward to doing so. Be positive and tell that you're looking forward to sharing your story. Mention a couple of highlights from your presentation: saying some ideas out loud helps you get your voice working and moves your mind into gear.

This will all reduce your stress levels and allow your body to be in control, to enable you to perform at your best. It's also much more useful than using the time to run through the slides one last time, which often only results in an increase in tension.

**LOCATION, LOCATION, WHERE'S THE LOCATION?**

# 7. Focus on your delivery more than the details

Back in 1967, psychologist Dr. Albert Mehrabian published two research papers assessing what elements of a presenter's communication had which impact. His conclusion was that the impression consisted of;

- 7% verbal (the words the audience hear and read)
- 38% tone of voice (how the presenter speaks)
- 55% body language (what the presenter does)

Mehrabian's research has been criticised and questioned over the years. For sure, anyone who loves to load their slides with details and explanations will contest this data furiously. *How am I supposed to get my message across without explaining it in words on my slides?*

Yet Mehrabian's theory is a very strong guide regarding quantity of content. Yes, the words do matter, but what the audience will go away with primarily is an impression of you as the presenter. How you said it will be more memorable than what you said.

In reality, you can rarely get a complete story over in a 15-20 minute presentation. What you can deliver is the headlines, and an incentive to find out more if they need to. A concise, well-delivered and confident presentation will always be more memorable than a complicated story of endless content and duration.

THEY WON'T REMEMBER
A WORD YOU SAID

There are numerous resources enabling you to share detailed follow up information: intranet, email, company server, etc. Colleagues can pick up the slides and additional documentation any time they like.

What colleagues can't do later is hear it from you, which gives them so much more. What's the attitude behind this project? Who is the person leading that team? What kind of entrepreneur am I being asked to invest in?

So before starting that first PowerPoint slide, bear in mind that the timeless 'Less is More' approach is hugely relevant for most presentations.

Ultimately, the slide content should provide cues for you, to know what you're going to say next; and cues for your audience, supporting your words and actions, and helping them follow the story.

### Three to remember

1. Keep the content concise.
2. Focus on how you will deliver your story, as much as the details of the message itself.
3. Provide the option to receive more detailed content on request.

# What you do speaks so loud that I cannot hear what you say.

Ralph Waldo Emerson
(philosopher)

# 8. Test-drive your talk

Chances are that you're being asked to present about something you've spent a lot of time on. You've probably talked about the subject many times with your colleagues in informal meetings, in planning sessions and especially at the coffee machine.

I advise: keep talking.

When you verbalise the issues you're dealing with every day, you find your language to distil that work into short sentences and concepts. You develop a vocabulary of work, a 'phrase-toolkit' of how to explain what you do.

You can also test out whether people 'get it' or not because you'll see it in their faces. Pay careful attention to reactions: and if they don't get it, ask them, "I'm not sure I'm explaining this too well, what's not clear here?"

Refining your vocabulary, phrases and concepts based on what people understand in informal discussions is a perfect way to prepare for a presentation.

Don't wait until there's a presentation to be made. Test-drive your story in every situation you can find.

SPEND TOO MUCH TIME
AT THE COFFEE MACHINE

# 9. Use PowerPoint as a tool and consider other options

PowerPoint gets a bad press: the common phrase, *Death by PowerPoint* is an example. I believe the problem lies not with the tool itself, but rather in what presenters do with it.

Note the word 'tool'. A piece of software does not make a presentation, it only provides a tool for you to deliver your message. You can choose to use it as you will. And probably, you'll want to avoid the top mistakes made in making PowerPoint presentations.

We've all seen it. Animation for non-epileptics; bullet-points for detail addicts; 200 word quotes that fill the slide; charts with hundreds of numbers, requiring binoculars from the second row back; and the 57 slide presentation for a 15 minute slot that has the presenter saying after 30 minutes, "Time is tight, I'll skip this one." (*Hmm, why is it there if you could skip it…?*)

For those who have a strong aversion to PowerPoint, or are looking to make an especially creative presentation, you can choose some clever alternatives. A series of handwritten flip-charts can be a very powerful way of communicating, especially if you hang them up around the room before everyone arrives. This enables the audience to see the whole story and refer backwards and forwards to your logic, as well as the conclusion.

If you're really adventurous, simply pinning a few pictures

**POWERTOOLS**

on the wall and talking through the issue based on the images can leave a long lasting impression.

Another method to try out is Prezi.com. It's a creative online tool that helps you get more of an overview-oriented message across. If your area is sales, try Clearslide.com, which is especially good for sales pitches.

Using something different conveys a message about you and a willingness to be unconventional. If that's what you want to communicate, and you feel confident to do it, go ahead. Nevertheless, around 90% of presentations are made using good old PowerPoint.

So my advice is this: until you are very confident in presenting, stick to the standard medium. It's what audiences are used to and if you follow some basic guidelines on how to construct your presentation (which we're about to come to) you can make it work well for you.

There's one concept to give some thought to, however, before we start getting words and images down on the page.

### Three to remember

1. PowerPoint is the universal presentation medium: use it as a tool for you to convey your message, not as the message itself.
2. Consider other tools once you are experienced and confident in front of a group.
3. Prezi.com or simple flip-charts are alternatives.

If your words or images are not relevant, making them dance in colour won't make them more relevant.

Edward Tufte
(Yale professor)

# 10. Use the Power of Three

There is a certain magic about the number three.

There seems to be no rational explanation why: it's just out there in so many ways that we simply cannot ignore it.

Western society has been influenced by the ultimate trinity; The Father, the Son and the Holy Ghost. When Cicero was perfecting the art of oratory in Ancient Rome, the Latin phrase 'Omne Trium Perfectum' was key – meaning 'everything that comes in threes is perfect.' Lincoln said in his Gettysburg address, "A government by the people, for the people, and of the people."

There. That was in threes. It's just more persuasive, isn't it? And here are a few more examples.

Ready, steady, go! Lights. Camera. Action! Veni, Vidi, Vici. (I came, I saw, I conquered.)

Three Blind Mice. The Three Musketeers. The Three Stooges.

"Three things cannot be long hidden: the sun, the moon, and the truth." Buddha. "I'll try anything once, twice if I like it, three times to make sure." Mae West. "There are three kinds of lies: lies, damned lies, and statistics." Benjamin Disraeli.

So how do we apply this to presentation? Simple: never put more than three pieces of information in front of your audience at any one time.

Hard to believe your heavily detailed work can be expressed so simply. Yet breaking down your presentation

**POWER OF THREE**

into parts of three is a highly effective method of ensuring your audience understands and remembers the message.

The good news: you can break your threes down into further threes. Here is one example;

You're presenting the sales of a certain product and want your management to invest more money and energy into marketing to back your winner;

> Your key message: We should invest in product Z.
>
> Your storyline: a. Business of this product is growing, b. However market share in not as strong as we'd targeted, c. We can gain extra turnover by investing more.
>
> Your arguments: a. 60% of the market is in 3 countries; b. If we gain 5% market share in each, we'll reach our European target; c. The cost of this investment will be X.

It is absolutely guaranteed that if you stick to the power of three, your presentations will be more memorable, more actionable and more appreciated.

## Three to remember

1. Use the Power of Three to your advantage.
2. Show a maximum of three pieces of information at any one time.
3. You can add three sub-points to each of your three main points.

# No-one can remember more than three points.

Philip Crosby
(businessman)

# 11. Put your presentation together on Post-it notes

You've been allowing your mind to wander over this subject and letting yourself think about the core of your key message. You've taken the power of three seriously and are breaking down in your mind some of the sentences and concepts you want to deliver.

The natural next step might be to open up PowerPoint, load the corporate template and start with Slide One. But there is something flawed about this approach.

For you to make the presentation hang together, you need an overview of the whole story. The classic Beginning, Middle and End must connect firmly together so the audience go away thinking, *That whole thing made sense.*

How can you achieve this when you only look at one slide at a time? Forget the reflex to power up the computer and try something new.

Lay your hands on a few sheets of A3 paper, some Post-it notes, and ideally a few differently coloured markers. Now (very important) turn off the email and smartphone, sit somewhere quiet and allow yourself to get focused.

Begin by addressing your main issues. What three things do you want them to remember and take action on from this presentation? Don't forget the power of three, and the fact that they will not remember much actual content – they'll remember the way you delivered it.

POST IT TO YOURSELF

Then write each key point in a different colour on separate Post-it notes and stick them on separate pieces of A3.

Now you can start filling in further content. Don't do this in any particular order: just write down phrases and ideas related to your presentation's subject and place the Post-its randomly on the A3 paper.

Spread out the sheets so you have an overview of what you are getting down, because that will spark new ideas. Move the Post-its around to re-organise as much as you feel is necessary, clustering them around the three key messages.

Don't think too hard. Just write out what comes to mind, and get it down. Keep it short and don't write in complete sentences: stick to a few key words or important phrases. And if you're feeling really creative, throw in a few rough drawings and diagrams to illustrate the message.

Once you've put down a lot of your ideas, take a step back and look at the connections between what you've written on the stickers. An order will start forming, and you'll begin to see how one issue leads to another. Now you're developing a more complete view of the presentation.

You'll find this method helps release your creativity way more than the 'start with Slide One' approach. Here's why.

When you work on PowerPoint, you're doing a huge number of technical things related to the software itself. You're trying to get the font size right, make the graphics line up, ensure the Agenda is complete, work out how to do that (probably unnecessary) bit of animation, worrying why Microsoft put your favourite button in another place in their latest update…

Plus, you're sitting at your desk – email, phone and

colleagues can all interrupt your flow.

How on earth can you focus on content like that?

Try out this new technique. You will completely surprise yourself at how much of your story will emerge from your head and onto the page in an incredibly short time.

Better still, you'll find yourself forming phrases that will appear in the presentation and you'll gain a clearer picture of the whole story, and that clarity will convey itself to the audience when you deliver the presentation.

The result will be a quicker path to reaching the core of your presentation; you'll lead the audience through your message as if it's a story; and they'll feel there is a conclusion and a clear reason why they are listening.

## Three to remember

1. Take yourself away from the desk, phone and email to give yourself enough physical and mental space for creative thinking.

2. Choose three key points and build your presentation around them.

3. Use the Post-it note method to get the content down quickly and to organise your ideas in a flexible manner.

*Preparation* | 49

# 12. Keep the details on your slides to a minimum

As we've acknowledged, PowerPoint is not in itself the presentation; it's a part of your platform from which you are going to present. The objective is for the slides to support your story.

Let's be clear on this: there is no need to tell your whole story in the presentation slides. You are going to do that yourself with your words, voice and attitude.

The purpose of your slides is primarily to provide the audience a guide to the story; and secondly to give you visual prompts for delivering your message.

It's hard for most presenters to imagine they will know what to say, or that the audience will get the message if there is little information on the screen. But I guarantee that you can always simplify your slides.

Take a look back at your Post-its. If anyone else looked at them, chances are they'd have a hard time deciphering the phrases and ideas you've scribbled down. However, if they asked you what each note meant, you'd have explanations for everything instantly at hand.

As you convert your Post-it notes into PowerPoint, keep this firmly in mind. In the slides, place concise expressions of what you want to communicate and, in parallel, spend time to think about the kind of words and phrases you'll use verbally to expand on them.

**DETAILED ENGINEERING**

Resist the temptation to expand into detail and simply think carefully through what you are going to say for each point. See the connections between the ideas in your message and express this in your slide content.

A classic and powerful method to avoid too many words is using an image instead. If you do, ensure that the image is relevant to your story and is an easy prompt for you to expand your message.

The stuff on screen is important, but not nearly as important as what you are going to say and how you are going to say it. That's why this book focuses heavily on your preparation and delivery, and less on what you are actually going to show.

Believe it or not, they're coming to see you, not your slides.

## Three to remember

1. You deliver the message, not your software.
2. Use images where possible and appropriate.
3. Think about what you want to say and use the slides to give concise prompts for you.

Once you get
the right image
the details
aren't that important

Abbie Hoffman
(activist)

# 13. Construct your slides: simple, clear, concise

If you work for any sizeable company, there will be a corporate template that you need to follow. If you're an entrepreneur, it's a good idea to make a consistent and standard format for your own company too.

Here's a straightforward list of do's and don'ts for slide creation: follow these and you won't go far wrong, giving you a solid basis of visual style for your message.

**Do;**

Remember the Power of Three as your guiding principle.

Use a very simple layout with minimal colours.

Include a small company logo: top left or bottom right.

Have an opening slide showing the presentation title, your name and your company name.

Make an agenda with three main points.

Use images to support your story where relevant.

Use a simple and common font (no Brush script or Plantagenet Cherokee). If the presentation is opened on a PC without your fonts installed, it will look terrible.

Use only one font; headings in bold, image captions in italic, the rest in regular.

Make type size at least 32 point.

Keep sentences short.

Use quotes, as long as they are relevant.

SIMPLE BEAUTY

Keep data and graphs as simple as possible, and highlight your key numbers.

Make a straightforward slide transition and apply it to all. 'Fade Through To Black' is best, set to 'Slow' in Options.

Run spell-check.

**Don't;**

Make five introduction slides. Get the listeners into the story as quickly as possible.

Use clichéd quotes. Adding a slice of Martin Luther King while launching your new Copier, Insurance package or iPhone App is simply inappropriate.

Bullet point everything (or indeed anything).

Make it too long.

Present graph after graph, sheet after sheet of Excel, with unreadable data.

Read the slides out to the audience.

Put every word you want to say on the slide.

## Three to remember

1. Keep it simple: minimise clutter to let your message stand out.
2. Be consistent in fonts, colours and logos.
3. Avoid small details to ensure the whole audience can read what's on-screen.

Everything should be made as simple as possible, but not simpler.

Albert Einstein
(scientist and genius)

# 14. Check out the equipment at the presentation venue

You need to be sure of what tools will be used at the presentation venue.

If it's a small meeting room and a one-off presentation, this is not so crucial. However, if it's a larger audience and you are just one of a number of speakers, there is much more to take into account.

Will you use your own laptop, or is there a central place to send your presentation in advance? In both cases, ideally use the break before you're on to make a quick check. Does your computer connect OK to the projector and the presentation show as you expect? Or does your presentation appear correctly on someone else's laptop that's being used for all files?

Often when you plug into a projector, there can be problems with screen proportions. For example, if you've set your presentation up in 4:3 format and the screen is 16:9, this will stretch your content, logo and images. Usually in such cases, there will be a technical guy to fix it. If not, try yourself for a couple of minutes at the maximum, but don't worry too much – it will still look OK.

If you've sent the presentation to someone else in advance, there is a possibility they will be using a different version of PowerPoint than you, which can cause some problems. Using standard fonts and avoiding excessive animation

**SPANNERS AT THE READY**

reduces most risk in this case as the majority of glitches will be in how the type appears and how the animation works. Have a quick look at 3-4 slides – you'll know straight away if there is a problem.

A small but important detail: if you're using a Mac computer to present with, make sure you have the adaptor cable to connect to the projector. It's annoying but true that Macs have a different connector from PC's. Any Apple Centre will have the right cable and adaptor.

Is there a lectern? Usually there is some kind of platform or table that has the presentation computer on it. We'll come on to your movement and body language later – for now, I would say that you can either do the presentation from behind the lectern or move around. Both have their benefits, and in general, it will be more dynamic if you move across the stage.

However, the lighting may be set up specifically so that you need to be behind the lectern to be seen – in which case, moving around is counter-productive.

If you do stay behind the lectern, you might have a temptation to grip hold of its sides for dear life! This is a clear signal to the audience that you are nervous, so just relax, stand up straight and deliver the story. Your hands should be free, ready to emphasise the key points.

Is there a microphone? And is it wireless or hand-held?

If it's wireless, then make sure you know how it will be attached to you. Is it going to be passed on from the previous speaker, or are there two mics so that you can attach it while the previous presenter is on stage? The second option is naturally better and easier, but if you do have to swap over, just take your time and don't hurry. The audience can wait for you to organise these small details.

If it's hand-held, you simply need to ensure you keep the microphone a good distance from your mouth so that your voice is picked up clearly – a couple of centimetres at the most is best. The difficulty is that you cannot hear whether the sound is being picked up or not so it is something you need to check in advance. Once you know the rough optimum position of the microphone, keep it in mind and do pay attention during your talk that your voice is being picked up.

Next let's talk about one important piece of equipment you should invest in for yourself.

## Three to remember

1. Ensure you're familiar with the equipment at the venue. Present from your own laptop if possible.

2. Microphone and lights are the two most important: they need to hear and see you.

3. Get there early and test out your presentation on the screen in case of compatibility issues.

# 15. Buy yourself 10% extra confidence

Before the days of laptops and beamers, we used to do presentations with overheads and slide projectors. It's truly hard to imagine, isn't it? Yet it was the only way.

My boss in the early '90s had a simple and very effective technique. He used a wireless control for advancing the slides, which he sometimes held out of sight behind his back. Without taking his eye from the audience, he would switch to the next slide and keep talking.

This approach was just one of the things that made him very convincing as a presenter. It felt like magic.

If you break it down, it's simple. He knew what was on the next slide and had a sentence in his mind for how to link the two slides: and he used a piece of equipment to enable the link to happen. Today, in theory this wouldn't work because he would have to walk back to the laptop and press a key to change the slide.

You can develop a high level of confidence yourself by taking action on all the steps you've read so far. Now there's a way to add an additional 10% of confidence by using a wireless remote control for your laptop.

There are a few available, and I leave the choice to you – most computer shops will stock a few different ones. Nevertheless, I must tell you that Logitech makes one that I

**CONFIDENCE TRICK**

have used for years that's simply excellent, called the R400. It's a little more expensive than others but it's worth every cent. It feels exactly right in the hand; you simply plug it in and it works (Mac or PC); and the buttons are very simple. Plus it has a laser pointer, enabling you to highlight key elements on your slides.

Being able to move the slides on without touching the computer simply makes you feel more confident, and the audience is always a bit mystified how you do it. They feel you are a step ahead of them, giving you an additional aura of authority, which in itself feeds your confidence.

### Three to remember

1. A wireless presenter will provide you with extra confidence and authority.

2. Practice using the wireless tool so that you can move effortlessly from one slide to another.

3. Logitech's R400 model is an excellent choice and will give you that 10% extra confidence.

# Anything's possible if you've got enough nerve.

J.K. Rowling

(author)

# Preparation: Summary

1. Give yourself enough time in advance to prepare and do a number of run throughs.
2. Spend at least 20 minutes of preparation per minute of presentation.
3. Take time to think about the profile of your audience and their expectations.
4. Know where the venue is and get there in plenty of time to be able to check the equipment.
5. Your delivery is worth more than the written content: invest time into practicing how you will tell your story, as well as in the story itself.
6. Test drive your ideas with colleagues at the coffee machine and learn which phrases and words work.
7. Use PowerPoint as a tool to communicate your message, and don't use it to over-complicate the visual style of your presentation.
8. Make the very best use of the Power of Three: break your information into threes.
9. Prepare using Post-it notes.
10. Leave your desk, switch off the phone and email, and give yourself time to think creatively about your story.
11. Keep your slides simple and concise and extract any complex or over-detailed information.
12. Buy yourself a remote control presenter and gain 10% extra confidence.

Our work is the presentation of our capabilities.

Edward Gibbon
(historian)

# Presentation

# 16. Gain confidence by visualising in advance

Take a look at this YouTube movie of a gymnast practising visualisation - tinyurl.com/3minvisualisation. You'll see how the gymnast rehearses her physical performance in her mind, concentrating on the process again and again.

Visualisation is a familiar technique to some. In case it's new to you, here's how you can apply it to your presentation.

It's about picturing yourself going through the steps towards success. Sit quietly the day before you're due to present and imagine yourself, in vivid detail, being introduced, walking to the front and delivering your first sentences. Try to make it as vivid as possible in your mind: the clothes you'll be wearing, the room you'll be in, some individuals who will be in the audience. Think about the best moments of your speech and how you'll deliver them.

Finally, visualise the end of the presentation. Your last slide comes up; you give a clear and succinct summary of your message; and you thank the audience. They clap, you take the applause, and you walk off, satisfied.

It's perhaps strange to think that playing it through in the mind can help in reality. But for some reason, it just works.

# SPORTSMAN'S MENTALITY

# 17. Keep calm if you make mistakes

One misconception is that audiences are very critical. Yet in 80-90% of cases, the listeners will be positive towards you as a presenter.

Let's face it: most of them are happy to be in their chair and not your shoes. Many have experienced what it is to be the one presenting. The collective will of an audience is right behind you, wanting you to succeed. They're hoping all goes well for you and are looking forward to giving you a round of applause at the end.

This positive support is especially important to remember if you make a mistake. An audience understands that mistakes can happen, just as long as you don't make them feel uncomfortable about it.

If you drop something, simply smile, pick it up and carry on. Mumbling something like, "Blast, I always do that! Why am I so clumsy?" makes the audience feel edgy. If you press the wrong button on the computer or a movie in your presentation doesn't show on-screen, turn to the audience with a smile, say something simple like, "That wasn't meant to happen!" turn away and fix the problem.

If you can't fix it (which will only happen rarely if you did the checks as mentioned), tell them "Something's not quite right with that movie, I'll send a link to you later. What it demonstrated is..." and carry on with your story.

**WHOSE SIDE ARE THEY ON?**

There is one worst-case scenario to be ready for. You get up on stage, and something goes fundamentally wrong with the equipment, through no fault of your own – the beamer lamp blows, the computer's completely crashes, or the lights go out.

In this case, simply wait. If there is a technician around, don't worry - he'll fix it. In that case, tell the audience calmly "Something's gone wrong - we'll fix that right now." Go to the side of the stage, wait until the techie does his job, walk back to the stage and pick up the presentation as if nothing had happened.

If it's something you can fix yourself, then take your time. Tell the audience, "I'll just be a few moments" to let them know they need to wait. Don't hurry, re-set the equipment in your own time and away you go.

Preparation will reduce the possibility of things going wrong. A calm reaction if things do go awry will make the audience remember what did go right and forget the bits that didn't.

### Three to remember

1. Don't worry if you make a mistake: the audience will be patient and on your side.

2. If something technical goes wrong, stop and fix it (or let the technician sort it out.)

3. Reduce the chance of things going wrong by preparing and checking the venue's equipment.

I am the most spontaneous speaker in the world because every word, every gesture, and every retort has been carefully rehearsed.

George Bernard Shaw
(writer)

# 18. Ensure they remember the important stuff

The reality is, the audience has many things on their mind; a meeting later on, an important email that just popped up on their smartphone, personal problems - you name it. Sitting still for 20-30 minutes means they will naturally start to mull those things over and their focus can drift.

During the Post-it Note process, you've established the key messages you want to get across. Here are two simple tools to ensure the audience remember them.

Firstly, give the audience very clear signals to pay attention at certain moments, so that you keep the audience alert. Be specific during your presentation about these core messages by telling them "There are three key points I want you to remember today. If you go away with nothing else from this presentation except these three, I believe we'll be taking a step forward. Now here's the first point."

On the slides introducing the important issues, make a visual mark to ensure they understand that this is something they really need to remember. It can be as simple as a light bulb, a brightly coloured shape, or a photo of a notepad. Use the same image for each of the three important issues so that you are consistent and clear.

Re-enforce it with your body language. As you tell them, "There are three key points," put your hand up with all your fingers stretched out. Next say, "Here's the first."

**MEMORY TEST**

Put your forefinger out with your hand up to make clear you are referring to the first one. Repeat this for each of the main points as you come to them during the presentation.

You'll be amazed how often people get their pens at the ready when you do this, and it will also help you to structure your presentation.

## Three to remember

1. Go back to the Post-it note exercise to find the most important points.

2. Give clear visual cues with your body language when there are key issues to be remembered.

3. Place a visible signal on your slides to indicate to the audience that they should take special note.

# We shouldn't abbreviate the truth but rather get a new method of presentation.

Edward Tufte

(educator)

# 19. Don't learn your script

It is a natural temptation to learn what you plan saying. After all, you know you'll feel under pressure up there in front of the audience – what could give you more confidence than memorising your message?

However, this idea is fundamentally flawed.

Most presenters speak at around 120-140 words per minute. If you have to learn a 25-minute presentation, that's around 3,500 words. Doesn't sound too much, does it? Well, to put it in perspective, that's the equivalent of the first act of Macbeth, or three times the length of John F. Kennedy's inaugural speech.

Check the movie on YouTube (tinyurl.com/3minJFKspeech): you'll see JFK didn't bother to learn it either.

If you try to do memorise a presentation lasting over 10 minutes, you will almost certainly forget a part of your script. If you are fixed on a certain text, when you lose the thread it's a struggle to get back. And if you do manage to memorise it, there's a chance you'll come across as non-spontaneous and insincere.

The good news is this. If you've followed the steps of preparation there is absolutely no need for you to learn what you plan to say.

Remember the Post-it notes and how you concisely summed up your main subjects? Your presentation content on-screen is giving you the same – key words and images to prompt you into the next step of your persuasion.

LEANING POSTS

Remember the coffee machine talks you've had about the subject? Those chats arm you with a series of standard phrases and sentences that are ready to come out.

And remember how much (or rather, how little) verbal content the audience will retain? What matters is getting your message across with confidence and prompting them to look for the details later.

Nevertheless, you do need some solid leaning posts across the presentation.

Think about those three things you certainly want them to go away with and remember at the end of your talk. It is worth having a couple of sentences that you know you will definitely say on those subjects. The best way to develop your phrases is through discussing the topic with others in advance of the presentation.

And there is one very important exception to this rule, which we'll come to in the next chapter.

### Three to remember

1. Don't try to memorise your script: it's almost impossible and can cause you to lose your way.
2. Keep the coffee machine talk going to prepare and test-drive your story.
3. Do have a few sure sentences for your most important points, as leaning posts and structure for the rest of the presentation.

I'm not afraid
of storms, for I am
learning
to sail my ship.

Aeschylus
(playwright)

# 20. The first 60 seconds

The only part of your presentation that I recommend you to learn word for word is the first 60 seconds.

Consider what happens when you get up on stage. Your heart-rate increases. You probably begin sweating because your body temperature rises. Your hands might even shake a little. You're super conscious of every move you make and concerned that everyone can see your uncertainty.

This all takes place because your body reacts under stress and goes into 'fight or flee' mode. Instinct takes over and pumps your body full of adrenaline: your mind is less engaged and the animal need to prepare for an attack wins.

Even the most experienced presenter in the world will suffer from some level of stress at the beginning of a presentation, because it's a moment of being on show for all to see. It's hard to think straight when the body is reacting that way. You're under the spotlight – nowhere to hide.

There is nothing like hearing yourself deliver a few good lines to give you confidence. Learning the first 60 seconds will help bring your body back on your side.

If you get the first sentences out of the way, without having to think too much, everything starts to relax. Your instinct gets calmed, realising that the threat of attack is not so high. Your heart rate drops, your body temperature starts heading back to normal and any shakes evaporate. Then you can concentrate on communicating your message in the most convincing way possible.

**GONE IN 60 SECONDS**

I once forgot this and walked out in front of 300 people from all over Europe. I'd prepared the presentation meticulously and felt I had a good story with clear slides to support it, plus I had a few solid leaning-post sentences along the way that made me feel very confident.

Yet forgetting to rehearse the first 60 seconds made all that work evaporate. I walked out and said, "Good morning ladies and gentlemen – or rather, it's the afternoon, isn't it? Well, thanks for coming today, I know some of you, erm, most of you have flown in from a long way, so it's great that you're all here, having come so far. It's great to see so many nationalities represented, from near and far..." etc.

It was horrible: my heart rate stayed high, my voice got thinner and the audience got further and further away from me. No matter how much I'd prepared the whole thing, those first 60 seconds ruined it.

I've talked this over with many experienced presenters and even musicians and performance artists. They all say the same. The opening 60 seconds are the platform and basis for the rest of the presentation or performance.

### Three to remember

1. Every presenter suffers from stress, just like you.
2. Learning the first 60 seconds helps calm you down and get into the 'flow'.
3. Memorise only this first minute: it's enough to give you confidence for the rest of the presentation.

What I learned most was how to tell a story in 15 seconds or 30 seconds or 60 seconds - to have some kind of goal of what to try to do and make it happen in that time.

Renny Harlin
(film director)

# 21. Use body language to express yourself

In Chapter 7, you can read the formula of content, voice and body language that the audience will remember. This naturally leads you to focus on how you communicate with your voice and body to strengthen the story.

Most important is to prepare well. That will help you be relaxed and in control of your content and story, which will automatically convey itself to your audience.

Here are a few additional suggestions to add some strength to your physical communication.

At the beginning, walk out in front of the audience, stand up straight, take a second and smile. This delivers a clear signal to the audience that their attention is required. Keep as upright as you can without being stiff: remain relaxed and professional.

Find your own level of comfort regarding where you stand. There is research suggesting the best position is to the left of the screen (from the viewer's point of view) but this depends largely on how the room is set up.

Ideally you stand where your laptop is easily visible, so that you are able to read your content and see the slide transitions while looking at the computer, not the screen behind you. Turning your back on the audience should be done very rarely, and this laptop setup will help you.

If the audience is sitting in a U-shape, it can be quite

**YOU ARE THE STORY**

powerful for you to walk into the middle of the group during your talk. However, use this very sparingly – it can also be quite threatening for an audience member if you walk up close and talk directly to one person.

My suggestion is to walk a little closer to the audience when introducing yourself. Then find one, or at maximum two more moments during your talk when you can tell them something without referring to the slides, and do this a little closer to them too. A short personal anecdote works well in this way.

It's not essential to move around during the presentation, but if you decide to do so, be careful not to pace backwards and forwards: it causes the audience a lot of anxiety. Choose three spots in the room where you can effectively tell your story, and move between those spots at various moments during the presentation. Walk slowly and hold your attention on the audience, keeping them involved.

Unsure about this? Then remain in one place and concentrate on delivering the message with your voice and body language from a position of comfort.

## Three to remember

1. Preparation will give you a relaxed basis.
2. Position yourself so that you don't need to turn your back on the audience.
3. Present from one place, unless you feel very confident with moving around the room.

A blur of blinks, taps, jiggles, pivots and shifts... the body language of a man wishing urgently to be elsewhere.

Edward R. Murrow
(broadcast journalist)

# 22. Emphasise the message by using your hands in a conscious way

Your hands are perhaps the most important part of your body to pay attention to, because they can either be very useful or very distracting.

A first simple rule: don't put your hands in your pocket. The worst-case scenario is a pocket full of change, which you jingle unconsciously throughout. I know this seems obvious, but so many people do it that it has to be said. Take out everything you don't need from your pockets; keys, tissues, money, receipts. They act like hand-magnets.

Be relaxed and you'll know what to do. When you come to a key point, use your hands to emphasise it. On a few occasions, point to the screen to make clear that this is something to remember. Do it sparingly and it has impact. Do it too much, with every slide and every message and the focus is lost.

There is one moment where you can consider putting a hand in the pocket; during a Q&A. It gives a signal that the formal part is over, and the audience is at liberty to put their questions forward. Do it with just one hand for parts of questions session, and only if it feels comfortable (and if there's not a single stray penny in there.)

**YOU NEED HANDS**

One no-go is the politician's hand position – think Tony Blair. It's a symmetrical shape of the arms, elbows out, with the tips of the fingers touching together or partly entwined. We are trained now to know that this position is that of the smooth talker trying to cover stuff up (or the *B*liar...) Avoid this position at all costs.

Using your hands also improves your vocal expression. Voice actors use their hands to fill their words with additional emotion, because no-one can see their body language.

To see how your hands can express emotion, try saying the following phrase with your hands clasped firmly together. "I had a great weekend. I met with some friends and we had such a laugh!"

It just doesn't work, does it?

Now think about how you explain things in the pub. If you tell someone about your weekend over a drink, you do it with hands and emotion. Let that happen in your presentation too.

If you put these tips into practice, you'll add a new dimension to your communication.

## Three to remember

1. Keep your hands out of your pockets, and empty your pockets in advance.
2. Point to the screen sparingly to emphasise your message and key moments.
3. Avoid the politician's hand-clasp.

> Enthusiasm is the sparkle in your eyes, the swing in your gait, the grip of your hand: the irresistible surge of will and energy to execute your ideas.
>
> Henry Ford
> (inventor)

# 23. Break through the voice barrier: listen to yourself

Almost everyone says, "I hate hearing my voice" if they're played a recording of it. It's a curious issue but there is a reason for it.

When we speak, we hear the sound in our own head. In recording and being heard by others, our voice's sound waves are subject to various influences of environment as they travel through air.

The result when hearing a recording is our voice sounds quite different to what we think is heard when we speak. Our dislike comes from the confusion caused by that difference between what we think we hear, and what happens while we're recorded.

Don't worry about any of this. Your basic voice is a part of who you are and will sound great to most, not so great to a few. What matters is what you do with it: here are some suggestions to help you.

**Be loud enough to be heard.**
If you use a microphone, check the tips in Chapter 14. If not, make sure you speak at a level that's audible for the whole audience. Ask a colleague to sit at the back and indicate if you're loud enough or need to add some volume.

**Monotone is the enemy.**
Record your voice (yes, be brave and break through the hate barrier) and see if there is a good variation in the

STEREO

tone of what you say. Refine how you emphasise certain key words, and ask yourself if there are better ways to do it. Re-record your voice and try different approaches: for example, record one time with your hands still, and another moving your hands around. You'll find the difference quite significant. Try one part louder, another part softer: one part higher, another part lower.

**Pay special attention to how you round off sentences.**
Keep the energy to the last full stop. Often the most important word is the last one in the sentence, so make sure they can hear it clearly.

**Find three or four occasions in the presentation where you make a clear 'moment'.**
Stop for a second. Take a breath. Tell the audience, 'So, we've covered XYZ. Now what I'd like to talk about is...' and make sure that this has a clear emphasis. This is like reading a long paragraph in a book – it's almost a relief when you can come to the next one. The page-break helps you read, and this breath-break will help them listen.

## Three to remember

1. We don't like our recorded voice simply because it sounds different to what we hear as we speak.

2. Record yourself several times, listen and refine.

3. Stop for a second at a number of points in the presentation, giving the audience some breathing space to re-focus their attention.

Words mean more than what is set down on paper. It takes the human voice to infuse them with deeper meaning.

Maya Angelou
(poet)

# 24. Share your eye contact

Have you ever sat in a meeting with a number of people, and found that the main person in that meeting looks at everybody but you? Did you ever go to a party as a couple and find that someone took no interest in you and only talked to your partner? It makes you feel excluded and unimportant – and that's exactly how you don't want anyone in your audience to feel.

Making eye-contact is a simple way of telling someone, "You are included, you are a part of this." Equally, focusing too much on one or two listeners is likely to make them feel uncomfortable, and to make others feel excluded. How you share your eye-contact with the audience is a crucial way of getting them involved, and communicates that you are calm and in control.

The formula is straightforward: try to include the whole room during the course of the presentation, and do it in a relaxed way.

Each time you say something, it's broken up into chunks as either short sentences, or parts of longer ones. Look at one person and begin speaking; when you come to a good break, glance to another part of the room, look at another person and finish the sentence. Then move to another person and continue. Keep their eye for a few seconds at a time and move on again.

It might sounds a bit contrived, but if you try it out a few times, it will quickly become natural.

**EYE TO EYE**

# 25. Make it interactive once you've gained confidence

Advanced presentations are not just a delivery to the listeners – they are an interaction between the presenter and the audience. It's not an easy technique, and I recommend to get the basics in place first. However, once you are finding confidence and have given a number of satisfying presentations, it's time to consider adding interaction.

Questions are the key, yet they can be both very powerful, and extremely problematic.

The worst kind is open-ended, where it might be possible for an audience member to talk endlessly on the subject. "Does anyone have an opinion on global warming that they'd like to share?" Cue passionate 10 minute monologue on the issue from someone the audience have not come to hear.

The best question is the one where you know the possible answers. For example: "Who believes Global Warming is an important issue for today's society?" In this case, you need to tell the audience what to do – it's horribly cringing for all if you ask and nobody answers. If you want them to say something, tell them so. "Shout out 'Yes' if you agree". If you want them to put their hand up, put your own hand up and tell them to do the same.

And here's a tool to help take your presentations to the next level of interaction.

**PRESENTATION 2.0**

# 26. The standing up game

I saw a guy called Daniel Frances do this at a Cold Call seminar, and the resulting interaction was the highest I have ever seen.

Daniel explained that he would make a statement, and the audience should stand up if it applied to them. The key to this technique is to be as inclusive as possible: therefore he began with, "If you're a human being, stand up". Naturally, everyone stood, helping them overcome their intrinsic fear of audience participation.

Then he asked, "If you've made a cold call in the last month, stay standing." It was a Cold Call seminar, so Daniel knew it was guaranteed that at least 60-70% of the audience would remain on their feet. He asked a question which got an answer he was expecting.

He followed up by asking who had made Cold Calls that day, knowing this would narrow it down: then he asked one of the remaining people to give their name, explain briefly what the call was about, and why it was important. Daniel picked out someone that he'd spoken to before the event began, that he knew would be comfortable with taking the microphone and giving their one-minute story.

He then asked two more people to do the same, moving to different parts of the audience.

During his seminar, Daniel followed this process on two more occasions. What happens is a change of dynamic. The audience moves from fear to involvement, with the

**ANY HUMAN BEINGS IN THE HOUSE TONIGHT?**

result that people were waving and actively grabbing the microphone by the final round of questions.

The power of this approach is in the audience telling the story. If they explain why the subject matters, and what the problems are that they need solving, the audience feels connected to each other and the presenter.

It also gives the presenter a few hints for subjects to pick up on in a later part of the event, and he can refer back to particular points made by the audience.

Try this tool out and you'll find yourself becoming more comfortable with introducing interaction into your presentations.

*Daniel is a special guy – check him out at thecoldcallcompany.com.*

## Three to remember

1. Start with wide and inclusive questions so the whole audience can participate.
2. Give people the chance to say their name and what they think the subject is important.
3. Letting the audience tell the story is a powerful way of involving them.

Involving the audience is a delicate thing. They came to see you do your work, yet they want their voice heard too.

David Beckett
(presenter)

# 27. How to manage a Q&A session

In general, it's good to build in time for questions, but as with the previous chapter, it's another situation that can go terribly wrong if you're not properly prepared. Here are a few tools to keep up your sleeve and stay in control.

**Someone asks a very negative question.**
Don't defend. Acknowledge the comment and focus on the positives of your message. If the questioner insists on responding negatively again (which happens in very few cases) suggest that you take the subject for discussion during coffee, and make sure you do. The person may just have a very valid point that you missed, which you can address in your next presentation.

**An audience member talks and talks.**
Stay calm, let them have their say and think about your answer – which ideally should be very short – while they are speaking. If they ask three questions in one, answer one of the questions, and if pressed for time, recommend to discuss the other two later or by email.

**Don't say, 'Good question'.**
They are all good questions because somebody having the nerve to speak up is already a good contribution to your meeting. Say, "thanks for your question" or something similar, to every question raised.

Q&A

**Never criticise the audience.**
Once I saw a presenter ask, "Who knows what coaching is?" A boy of around 17 raised his hand and gave his view: the presenter jumped in with, "No, no, no, that's a big mistake! Let me tell you what coaching really is…" The lad shrivelled into his seat, humiliated.

Even if an audience member says something off-track or plain wrong, tell them, "That's a way of looking at it." Then add your own steering of the subject back towards where you want your message to go.

**Keep questions to a very few.**
It can be gruelling to be up-front and handling questions. I would recommend five or six at most, and when you've reached five, make it clear you're about to end: "I'll take this question and one more, then we'll wrap it up."

If they clearly still have more to ask, advise them to send by email or to approach you afterwards. Being accessible is important: it makes clear that you genuinely want the audience to take action on your message.

### Three to remember

1. Opening up to the audience can be powerful but is also risky: be prepared.

2. Avoid arguments at all costs. If a contentious issue is raised, suggest that you discuss it during the break.

3. Keep it to around five questions.

A wise man can learn more from a foolish question than a fool can learn from a wise answer.

Bruce Lee

(actor)

# 28. Give handouts at the end, never at the beginning

Ideally your presentation should be clear, not requiring additional notes. Almost certainly, nobody will read handouts if you do provide them, unless you give them out at the beginning: a guaranteed way of ensuring the rustle of flipping pages drowns out your first 60 seconds!

There are, of course, exceptions.

On some occasions, you may want your audience to refer to detailed data during the presentation. In that case, I would recommend having the data on the slide and handing out prints of that specific slide, so that you don't have to read aloud every detail they can't see on the screen.

I also strongly recommend making two presentations; the one you personally deliver, and the one you distribute. The one you show should be light on data and detail, but the one you distribute may need to tell a more in-depth story, especially if you are sharing it with management as a reference paper. In that case, you can add the detail in their version, also helping you resist the temptation to throw every word and number into the slides you present.

Naturally creating two versions requires a lot of extra time and for most presentations is unnecessary. However, for the big ones, it's worth it.

DISTRIBUTE

# 29. Finish with a bang

Have you ever been to a concert where there was no encore? The band plays, gets up and walks off, giving the audience no chance to show their appreciation. It leaves you with a sense of unfulfilment, as if something's not quite complete.

I once talked with musician Tom Robinson, and he explained why.

"You've been up on stage and given the audience your best. Part of the process is that we as the audience like to say thank you in return. If the performer doesn't give us that opportunity, we feel like our part hasn't been played."

Tom also told me that the most important part of any song he played live was the end. "You can have an average song, but if you close it off with a clear riff and a bang, the audience will love it. They also need to know when to applaud, so give them a definite and clear ending moment."

Tom's tips can easily be translated into your presentation approach.

Firstly, make your summary interesting. Instead of having seven bullets that you read one by one, make it visual; choose an image or one single word to represent each main point. Rehearse this many times, as the last 60 seconds can be as important as the first.

Secondly, ensure you finish on a big issue; for example; 'And finally, we'll launch Product X in September, and the goal is to reach 10,000 sales by end of the year!'

ENCORE!

'To close off: we have three big projects to complete this year; first, complete transformation X; second, re-organise division Y; and third, reach sales of 5,000 with new product Z.'

Finally, be clear about the ending. After you say your last sentence, finish with a simple and firm, "Thank you!" Then stand and take the applause; in most situations, the audience will show their appreciation for you.

Of course, there is a risk that no one claps. That is a small possibility if you use these tools, but if it does occur, walk off after a couple of seconds and don't worry about it. You've done your job, and if the audience didn't get it...? Well, that happens sometimes. But only rarely, as long as you've done your preparation, created a strong story line, and finished on a high.

## Three to remember

1. Make the summary visual instead of a series of bullet points.
2. Be clear about when the presentation has ended.
3. You complete the process in a more memorable fashion by giving the audience a chance to thank you for your work.

# A good opening and a good ending make for a good film

Federico Fellini
(film director)

# 30. Follow up

You've done your preparation, delivered the message to the best of your ability, and the audience seemed to like it. The next part is what most presenters forget: the follow up.

Ideally, the audience understood the message, but how do you find out for sure? There are a number of ways.

Firstly, ask a couple of trusted colleagues to tell you the truth. What went well? What could be improved? What do they remember from the presentation? Try to get honest feedback at every opportunity, so that you can improve and refine details, personal style and clarity of expression.

Secondly, make sure to send the attendees a follow-up email, reminding them of the five most important issues. This is also an opportunity to send them a more detailed version of the presentation.

Finally, consider setting up an online questionnaire, especially if the audience numbered more than eight. You can find plenty of simple (and free) websites that offer this service; one that I use is SurveyMonkey.com. Keep the survey short and simple – maximum seven questions, with at least a couple of rating-related answers to fill in quickly, and a couple of general questions enabling attendees to spend more time to comment freely on how they rated your presentation.

Feedback is always useful and enables you to learn how your presentations are really being received.

# HOW WAS IT FOR YOU?

# Presentation: Summary

1. Take time sitting alone to visualise your presentation and success in advance.
2. Record and listen to your voice so you can improve the verbal aspect of your message.
3. Learn the first 60 seconds - not the whole script.
4. Stay calm if you make mistakes or if something technical goes wrong. The audience is on your side.
5. Give clear signals - both on-screen, in words and with your body language - as to which items are the most important for the audience to remember.
6. Present from one position until you feel confident enough to strat moving around.
7. Use your hands to emphasise the message, and keep them out of your pockets!
8. Share your eye-contact to ensure the whole audience feels included.
9. Make it interactive by asking questions: and only ask questions which will have answers you can predict.
10. Don't give handouts at the beginning. If you need to share detailed information, hand it out during the presentation, slide by slide - or send it afterwards.
11. Finish on a high note by making a clear motivational statement or a strong call to action.
12. Follow up with a short online questionnaire, so you can incorporate feedback into your next presentation.

**No one ever complains about a speech being too short!**

Ira Hayes
(soldier)

# Three Minute Presentation

# 31. You really can do all this in three minutes

You've gone through the book, acted on the advice that suits you best and applied it in a number of presentations. You're seeing improvements in your confidence, the quality of your content, and the reactions from your audience.

Now's the time to convert your skills and new knowledge into the ultimate: a Three-Minute Presentation.

You might ask yourself, "Why is this important?" It's because on some occasions you'll be called on to make the classic 'Elevator Pitch.'

You never know when you might be in the presence of an influential person for your project, career or own business. Generally those influencers will be busy people.

If you can get your message across in three minutes, the speed and efficiency alone is impressive and highly appreciated, because very few people can do it. You give a clear message: "I respect that you are busy so I'm adapting my story to your situation, not mine."

It sounds daunting. A presentation in just three minutes? But believe me: if you've followed the suggestions in this book, you already have all the tools required to do it.

**THREE MINUTE PRESENTATION**

# 32. Prepare an elevator pitch

First, go back to Chapter 11 and review the Post-it note method of preparation. Remember how it's all about finding the three main points and building from there? Use the Post-it note approach to prepared the structure of your short presentation.

Next, think again about the Power of Three. For each of your three main issues, you might be able to mention a maximum of three sub-points within the time available.

How to find them? Make sure you've done plenty of coffee-machine talk. The ability to describe concisely what you are working on is exactly what you've been developing while talking to your colleagues for snippets of two or three minutes.

You'll find if you look back that there are always a couple of killer messages that everyone just 'gets', and these should feature strongly in your short version.

In 90% of cases, this will not be a formal presentation with visual aides: your body language, attitude and tone of voice will make all the difference. Remember how little they will remember about the pure content? More than ever in the Three-Minute Presentation, your passion for your subject will have an influence on the audience response.

If for some reason it is in a formal setting, use images instead of lots of words. Single words or one short phrase on a slide can also be powerful, and the design of the slides should be as minimalist as possible. In three minutes,

**FORMULA THREE**

the amount of information displayed should naturally be limited. A maximum of three slides should be your guideline as that will focus your mind.

Here is a suggested formula;

> Tell what you are going to explain in one sentence.
> Break the subject down into three main points.
> Tell about the first, using a maximum of three sub-points.
> Do the same for the second.
> Do the same for point three.
> Finish with; "to summarise, the three main issues are…"
> Finally, close on a very clear call to action; "therefore I propose we invest x thousand in…", "based on this, our target market share should be X%, and we should invest in these three activities to reach it."

Write your content on Post-its, decide the three messages and their sub-points, and construct the bones of your Three Minute Presentation. Now you're ready to practice.

## Three to remember

1. The Post-it note exercise will remind you of your three essential points
2. Practice again and again one standard sentence that summarises your story in seconds
3. Give a clear call to action: what do you want them to do as a result of your pitch?

# No one can remember more than three points.

Philip Crosby

(businessman)

# 33. Practice makes perfect, again and again

Ideally, do the following exercise with a couple of trusted colleagues.

Ask them to open the timer on their phone with a loud alarm bell, set for exactly three minutes, and tell them to clap as soon as the alarm goes – no matter where you are in your presentation. Regardless of whether you are halfway through a sentence, or not even halfway through your whole presentation, they need to start clapping, stopping you in your flow.

Do a quick review to see how far you got, and to assess how satisfied you were with your pitch. Then do it again, straight away. And again.

After four or five run-throughs, you'll find you are getting closer. The pressure to shorten your sentences and get to the point is high when the clock is running and that can help replicate the pressure you'll feel when in front of a CEO or high-influencer. Ask your colleagues for honest, critical feedback to help you improve.

Another way to practice is to film yourself. It's brutal and hard to see yourself on camera, because you notice every odd movement and sound you make. But do it anyway: it's all in the interests of improving your pitch.

TIME'S UP

# Three Minute Presentation: Summary

1. Use the Post-it note technique to prepare.
2. Focus on the Power of Three to break your message down into three essential points.
3. Seek out the most effective words and phrases you've found while test-driving your talk at the coffee machine.
4. Practice one killer sentence that defines what you are proposing.
5. Be passionate and expressive.
6. Finish with a clear call to action: what do you want them to do next?
7. Try it out with colleagues and friends.
8. Film yourself to see how your presenting looks.
9. Set a timer and practice delivering your message within three minutes, again and again.

To write it took three months. To conceive it took three minutes. To collect the data in it? All my life.

F. Scott Fitzgerald
(author)

# Final Thoughts

# Get advice and feedback wherever you can

This book equips you with the most important tools to help you improve your presentation skills. You'll find some concepts mean more to you than others, depending on your personality and experience. I guarantee that if you put at least a few of these tools and concepts into action, you'll see a marked step forward in the way you feel about giving presentations, and the quality you deliver.

Yet any learning is a never-ending quest, and this area of development is no different.

Asking friends and colleagues for feedback on your presentations can be extremely helpful. In the words of advertising man Paul Arden: 'Ask for a slap in the face.' Yes, do get feedback on what went right, but it's often more useful to get clear and honest assessments of what did not go well, so that you can sharpen your weaker areas.

You can also seek professional advice. I offer coaching courses for individuals, small groups and larger seminar-style audiences, and will be happy to support you in developing your skills.

You'll also find a host of free resources at my website www.Best3Minutes.com to help support you in your progression. All pieces are readable in three minutes, so you can visit any time for a quick update.

**THREE MINUTE ADVICE**

# Additional presentation advice and resources

You can find all kinds of free advice and ideas about presentation at my website:
**Best3minutes.com/blog**

If you need coaching for your company's employees, I run tailor-made sessions face to face and by Video Conference.
**Best3minutes.com/presentation-coaching-for-companies**

A comical look at presentation: Don McMillan's movie at **tinyurl.com/3MinPresMistakes**

For an alternative way to make more engaging presentations, try out **Prezi.com**

See **Slideshare.com** for a huge database of presentations on numerous subjects

**Slideklowd.com** gives a whole new dimension to involving the audience in your presentations

An extraordinary 3 Minute Presentation:
**tinyurl.com/Great3MinPres**

Check **Presentain.com** for a great way to engage your audience more deeply in your presentations.

# Photo Credits
## ccf: Creative Commons Flickr
## wc: Wikimedia Commons

15. Andrea Sartorati (ccf)
17. Conrado Reis (ccf)
19. DFID - UK Department for International Development (ccf)
23. Alan Light (ccf)
27. MSG (ccf)
31. Wiki Commons (no attribution)
33. Adifans (ccf)
37. Silygwailo (wc)
39. Mike Beckett
43. Library of Congress (wc)
47. Tinkering Bell (wc)
51. Margaret Thatcher Foundation (wc)
55. Milton H. Greene (wc)
59. Unknown
63. Unknown
71. Dave Gilbert (wc)
73. Dodmedia (wc)
77. Sailko (wc)
81. Kheel Center, Cornell University (ccf)
85. United States Govt. Work (ccf)
87. gamp7783held (ccf)
91. Antonio Cruz (ccf)
95. Hans Bernhard (wc)
99. Allan Warren (wc)
101. Unknown
103. Daniel Francès
107. Greginhollywood (ccf)
111. British Government (wc)
113. Ham: londondailyphoto.blogspot.com
117. Jan Arkensteijn (wc)
123. LoveGreenPhotos (ccf)
125. Instituto Ayrton Senna (ccf)
129. Joost van Manen
135. Joost van Manen

*Three Minute Presentation* | 139

# Presentation is nine points of the law.

Lance Miller

(innovator)

# Get trained by TEDx speech coach David Beckett

Do you make presentations as part of your job? Do you ever wonder how the great speakers do it? And would you like to improve your presentation skills?

David Beckett has coached over 120 Startups, and hundreds of professionals to win investment and resources.

After working with David, you'll go away with tools to;

- Prepare and structure your talk in a creative way
- Capitalise on the Power Of Three
- Use voice and body language
- Calm your nerves and gain confidence
- Make a Three-Minute presentation on any subject

Courses are available on an individual basis, as well as for small and large groups.

**Email David at david.beckett@Best3minutes.com, or visit Best3minutes.com for further information.**

Made in the USA
Middletown, DE
14 May 2017